With love
and peace
Maria x

If...

Maria ★ Tarr

Antony Rowe Publishing Services

This book has been printed digitally and produced in a standard specification in order to ensure its continuing availability

Published by Antony Rowe Publishing Services in 2005
2 Whittle Drive
Highfield Industrial Estate
Eastbourne
East Sussex
BN23 6QT
England

ISBN 1-905200-05-6

Printed and bound by Antony Rowe Ltd. Eastbourne

Dedication

*To all the wonderful
people in my life who
have listened to my
endless stream of*
If's
*with infinite patience,
constant
encouragement and
unconditional love and
support.*

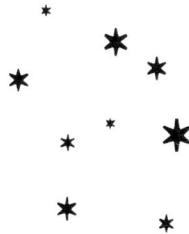

Acknowledgements

To all the special people in my life: my children, my yoga students and life coaching clients, my swimming friends and all those people who have encouraged and supported me. Also extra special thanks to Colin, Mel, John, Bernard and particularly Elizabeth, who has been amazing!

Last but not least my husband for being my rock, my PR man, my secretary, and for always being there to pick up the pieces when things go wrong.

If...

only

I

could

write

a

book...

If...

you look

into

my eyes

you

will know

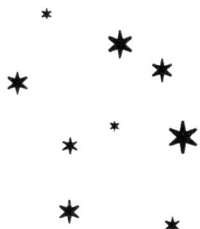 what

my

heart

is

feeling.

...I love you...I love...
you...I love you...
I Love you....
I Love you....
I Love you....
I Love you.... I Love you...
I Love you.... I Love you.....

If...

I could

express my

love for you

in writing

I would

run out

of paper

before I

ran out

of words.

If...

only

people

appreciated

the miracle

of the

human body

instead of

taking

it for

granted.

If...

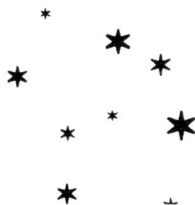

we think

something nice

about somebody

we should share it.

The thought

then becomes

a gift to

that person

and could

make their day.

If...

love and

encouragement

could be

packaged

in little boxes

and gift wrapped,

would the

shelves be

permanently

empty or full?

If...

you've

been

through

hell

everything

else

in life

seems

like

heaven.

If...

you

cannot

forgive

you

cannot

forget.

If...

you think

you can

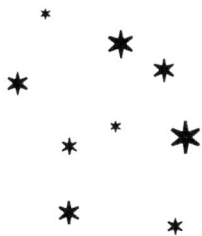

you are

absolutely

right.

If you think

you can't

you are

absolutely

right.

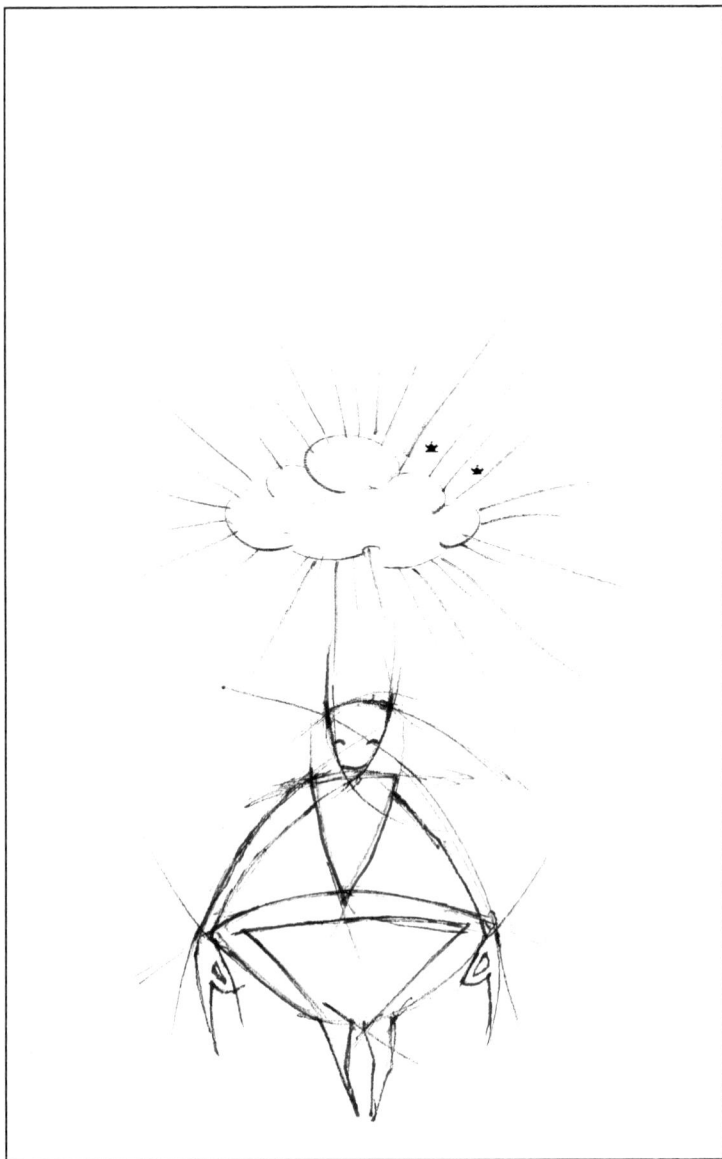

If...

only

my thoughts

could

heal

I would

sit

and

think

all

day.

If...

you

have

expectations

you

must

also

be

prepared

for

disappointments.

If...

you

assume

you

may

often

assume

wrong.

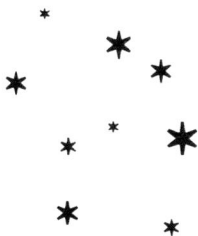

If...

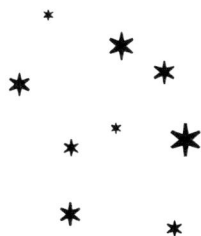

only

I

knew

then

what

I

know

now.

If...

only

I had

more

patience –

I'm working

on it

but it's

taking

such a

long time.

If...

you are

really

listening

you will

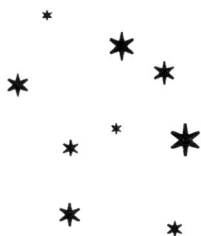

feel

the

words

as well

as hear

them.

If...

only

I

could

say

no

without

feeling

guilty.

If...

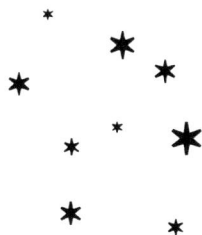

you

can

dream

it

you

can

do

it.

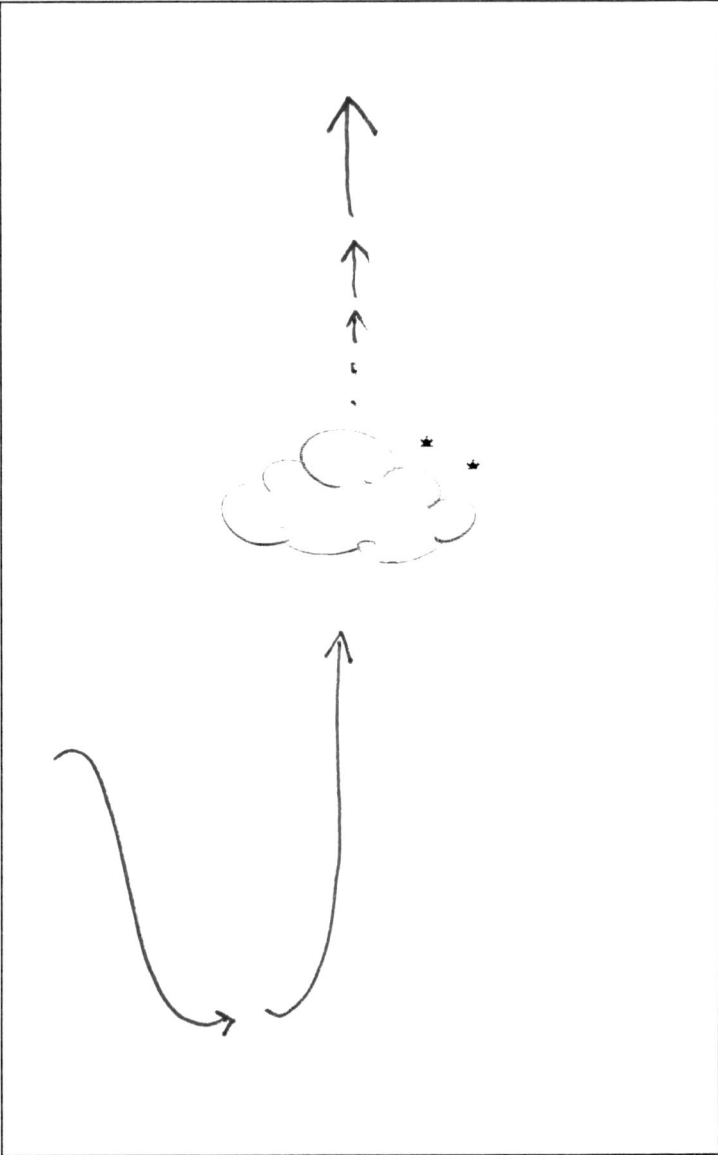

If...

you

are

down

the

only

way

is

up.

If...

you are

on the brink

it is better

than arriving

because once

you have

arrived all

you've got

to do is

leave.

If...

you

can't

do

what

you

love,

love

what

you

do.

If...

only

my

babies

didn't

have

to

grow

up.

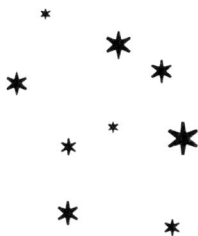

If...

only

we could

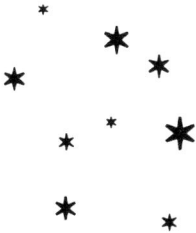

treat

others

in the

same way

as we

would

like to be

treated.

If...

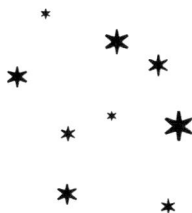

I could do

anything at all

that I wanted to

right now I would

have all the very

special people I love

here with me

in this room

and give them all

a big tight hug.

If...

you

could be

the best

in the

world

at one

thing

what

would

it be?

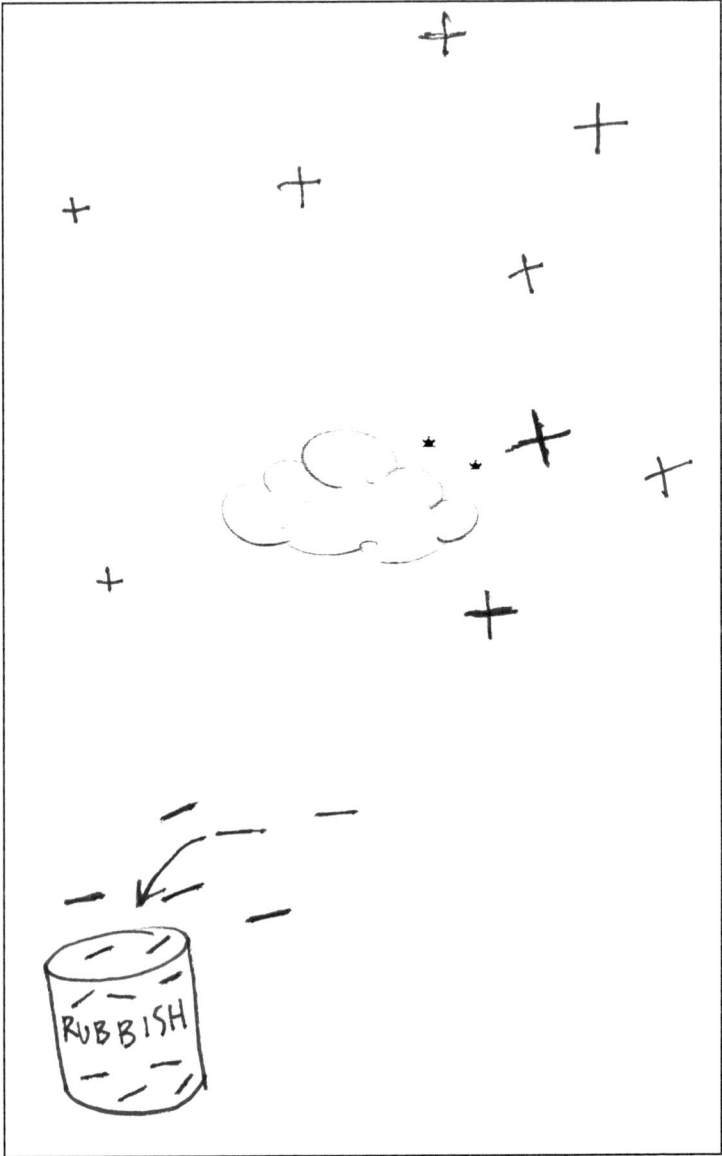

If...

you think

something

positive

give it

away.

If you think

something

negative

throw

it away.

If...

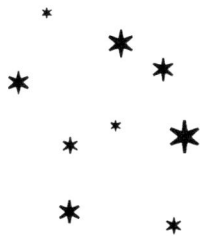

you

act

like a

closed

book

no one

will

want

to read

you.

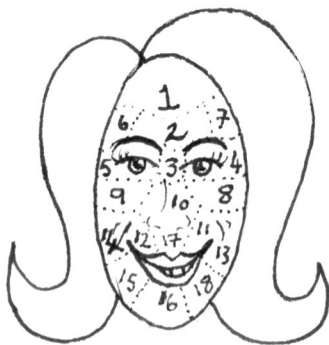

If...

only

people

were aware

it takes

fourteen

muscles

to smile

and

forty two

to frown.

If...

you

compare

yourself

with others

you

could

feel

superior

or

inferior.

If...

today

was the

last

day of

your

life

how

would

you

live it?

If...

you had

to choose

between

beauty

and

brains

which

would

you

choose?

If...

friends

were

flowers

I'd

pick

you.

If...

you

could

choose

to be

any

age

what

would

it

be?

If...

you

don't

get

what

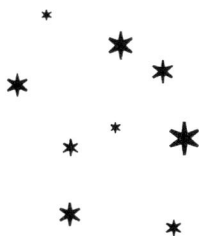

you

want

you

get

experience.

If...

the sea

ran dry

would

we

still

be

able to

build

sand

castles?

If...

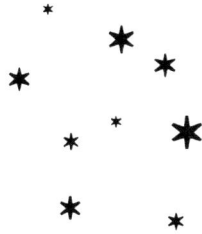

it were

possible to

read other

peoples minds

and you

had a

choice,

would you

say yes

or no?

If...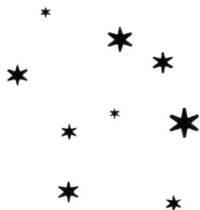

you were

asked how

'self confident'

you were and

what it would

take to

increase that

self confidence,

what would

your answer be?

If...

we

are

wise

we

will

know

what

to

overlook.

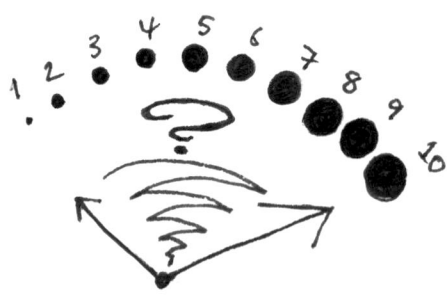

If... you had

to express

the overall

quality of

your life on

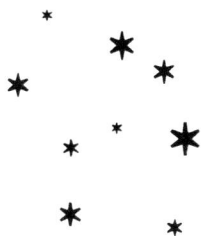 a scale of

one to ten

what number

would you

choose?

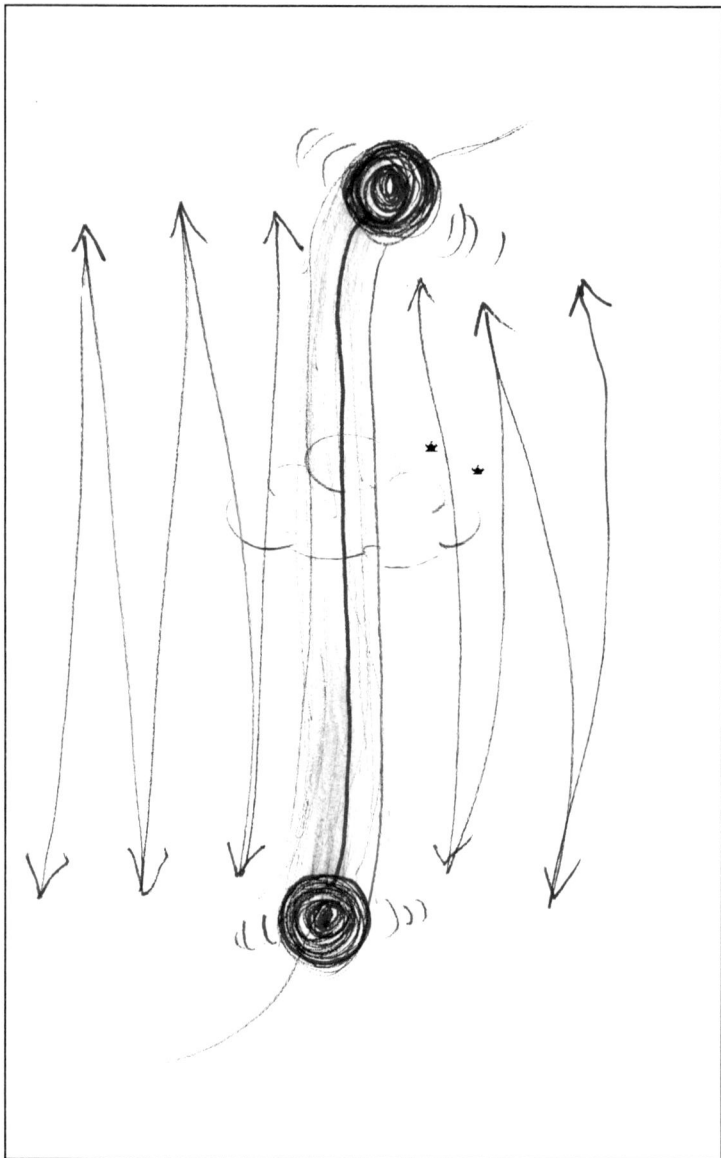

If...

you let

other peoples

opinions of

you affect

you,

you will

be up

and down

like a

yo yo.

If...

persistence

fights

with

failure

which

will

win?

If...

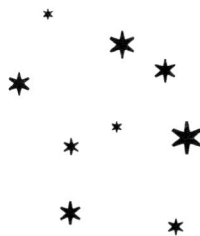

we

believe

in

acceptance

would

it

stop us

having

another

go?

If...

you

were

invisible

for

one day

what

sort of

things

would

you do?

can ~~t~~

CAN~~'T~~

If...

you

remove

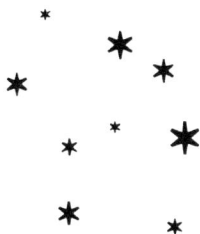

the

"*t*"

from

can't

you

have

a

chance.

If...

we only

had one

season

instead

of four

which

one

would

you

choose?

If...

you had

the option of

knowing exactly

the age time and

way you were

going to die

 would you

 choose to

know or

not know?

If...

we

were

totally

honest

would

that

be

good

or

bad?

If...

one person

gives you a

compliment

and another

a criticism

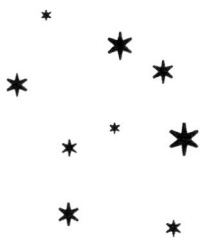

which

do you

hold on to

for the

longest?

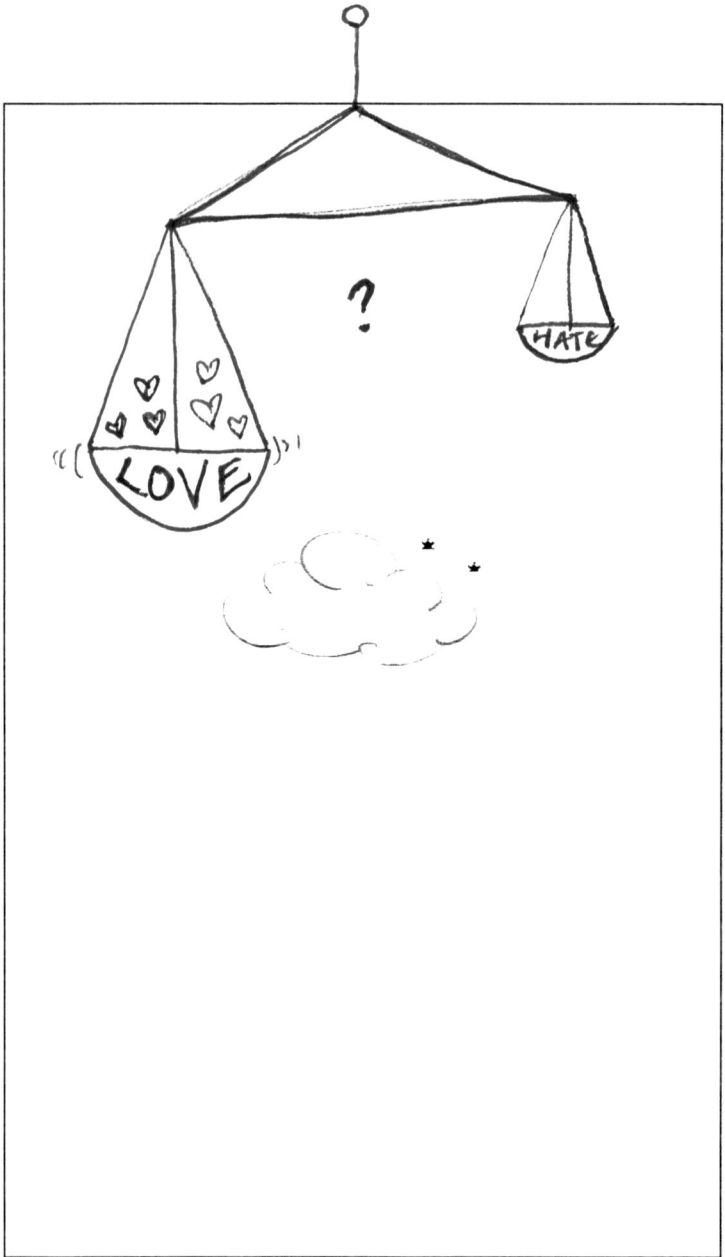

If...

It were

possible

to weigh

love

and hate

which do

you think

would

be the

heaviest?

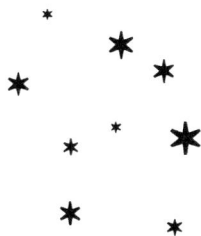

If...

you

keep on

doing

what you

are doing

you will

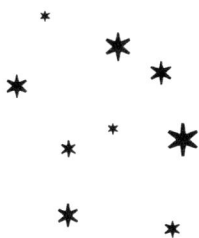

keep on

getting

what you

are getting.

If...

you give

somebody

a smile

give it

unconditionally.

If you

get one

back it

will be

a bonus.

If...

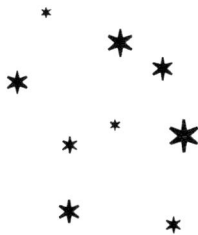

men

were

cups of

coffee

I'd have

mine

strong

dark

and

hot.

If...

you

cannot

have

what

you like

learn

to like

what

you

have.

If...

words

did

not

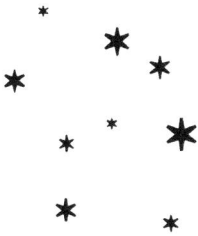

not

exist

how

would

we

communicate?

If...

you could

go back

in time

and do

things

differently –

would you –

and what

would

they be?

If...

       only

       I

       had

       time.

If...

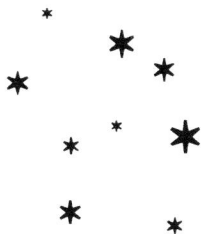

only

we

could

overcome

the

fear

of

fear

itself.

If...

you

had to

choose

between

being a

listener

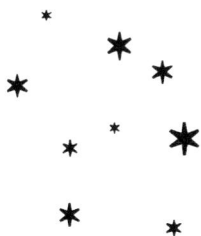

or a

talker

which would

it be?

If...

you

want

to

give

you

must

also

learn

to

receive.

If...

we

ask

the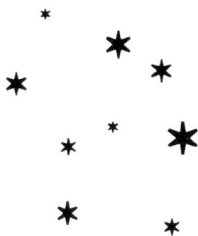

question

"how are you"

are we

really

interested

in the

answer?

If...

seeing

is

believing

what

is

faith?

If...

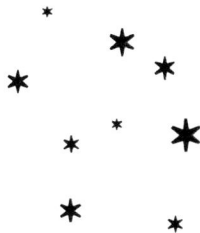

you

do not

believe

in yourself

how

can you

expect

others to

believe

in you?

If...

life is

full of

peaks

and

troughs

how do

we find

our way

to even

ground?

If...

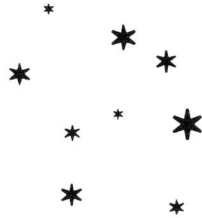

you

can

bend

you

are

less

likely

to

break.

If...

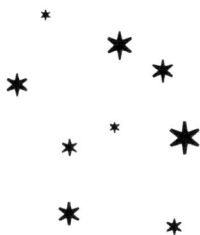

fear

were

to

have

an

antidote

would

it

be

hope?

If...

we share

our joy

will it

be

doubled?

If we share

our sorrow

will it

be

halved?

If...

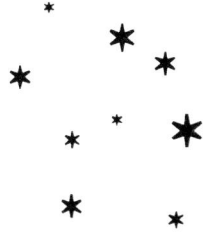

you

had to

choose

immortal life

or

natural life

what

would

you

choose?

If...

you

can't

be

tactile

try

a

smile.

If...

        it is

        nice

        to

        be

        important

        is it

        important

        to

        be

        nice?

If...

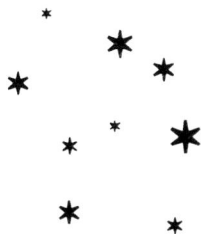

you

don't

have

a

go

how

will

you

ever

know?

If...

every

face

tells a

story

what

would

people

read

in

yours?

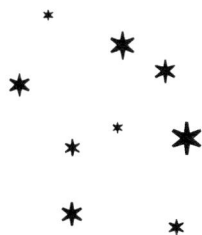

If...

we

let

go

is

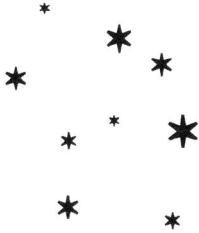

it

the

end

or a

new

beginning?

If...

we

expect

appreciation

are

we

giving

for

the

wrong

reasons?

If...

we are

always

up

how

can we

empathise

with

people

who are

down?

If...

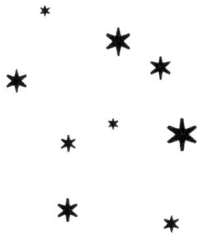

confidence

comes from

within

why do

we spend

so much

money

on our

outward

appearance?

If...

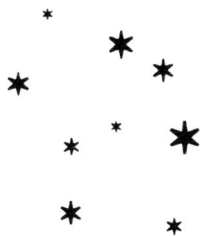

reading

is to the

mind what

exercise

is to the

body why

are the gyms

more popular

than the

library?

If...

you

could have,

do, or be

anything

you wanted

to, and be

a complete

success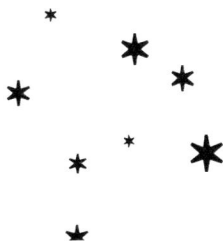

what

would it be?

If...

you

do

not

expect

anything

you

will

not

be

disappointed.

If...

you

have

respect

you

have

everything.

If...

you

cannot

be

the

best,

be

the

best

 you

can.

If...

everybody

followed

your

example

would

the

world

be a

better

place?

If...

you

had your

life

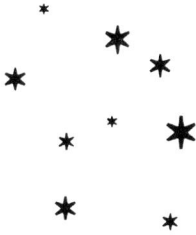

to live

over

once again

what

would

you do

differently?

If...

we

regret

we are

living

in the

past

instead

of

the

present.

If...

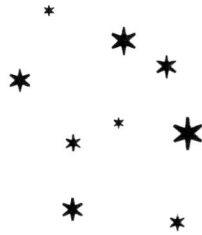

you

want to

overcome

something

you have

to go

through it

to reach

the

other side.

If...

you

hold

on

to a

grudge

you

hold

on

to

pain.

If...

air

inflates

a balloon

what

does

a

compliment

do for

our

ego?

If...

we

surrender

are

we

strong

or

weak?

If...

you

want

to

find

yourself

examine

your

baggage.

If...

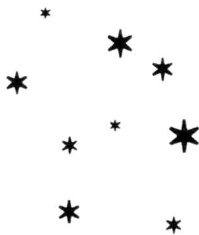

fear

holds

you

back

what

does

confidence

do?

If...

you

win

or

lose

do

it

with

dignity.

If...

you

fail to

write

down

your

thoughts

they

may

vanish

forever.

If...

only

I

had

taken

a

chance.

If...

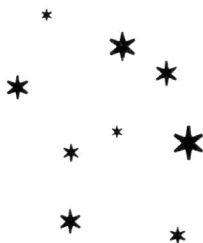

it

were

impossible

for

you

to fail

what

would

you

do?

If...

everybody

had the same

colour skin

and spoke

the same

language

would

the world

be more

united?

If...

we

see

obstacles

as

opportunities

life

becomes

more

exciting.

If...

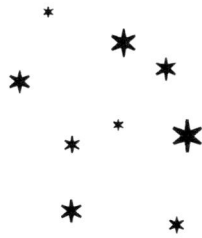

the

present

is

a

gift

what

is

the

past?

If...

you are

always

anticipating

the future

you are

missing out

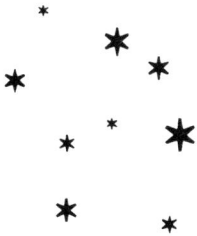 on the

present,

the here

and now.

If...

a

change

is as

good as

a rest

is a

rest

as good

as a

change?

If...

people

don't see

things

our way

is it

because

they are

looking from

a different

direction?

If...

you

were

asked

to write

your

own

epitaph

what

would

it be?

If...

these

make you

think

then I've

done

my job...

If...

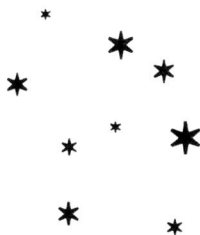

only I

could

write

a book...

and now

at last

I have.